Understanding John Steinbeck's Novel

Of Mice and Men

GCSE Study Guide

By Gavin Smithers

Another one of **Gavin's Guides** – short study books, packed with insight. They aim to help you raise your grade!

Published by Gavin's Guides

All rights reserved. No part of this publication may be reproduced or transmitted in any form or by any means, electronic or mechanical, including photocopy, recording or any information storage and retrieval system, without the prior written permission of the publisher.

Copyright Gavin Smithers, 2014

The right of Gavin Smithers to be identified as the author of this work has been asserted in accordance with the Copyright, Designs and Patents Act 1988.

This book is copyright material and must not be copied, reproduced, transferred, distributed, leased., licensed or publicly performed or used in any way except as specifically permitted in writing by the publishers, as allowed under the terms and conditions under which it was purchased or as strictly permitted by applicable copyright law. Any unauthorized distribution or use of this text may be a direct infringement of the author's and publisher's rights and those responsible may be liable in law accordingly.

Series Editor: Gill Chilton

The novel, Of Mice and Men by John Steinbeck (Penguin Classics, £8.99) is readily available on Amazon, in bookstores and from www.penguin.co.uk.

Let's Get Started

Steinbeck's "Of Mice and Men" has been a favourite text for GCSE for many years, for several reasons. It is not a long novel, and so it is quite easy to read; it is from America, and fits the "literature from other cultures" tag, and it has a range of interesting themes, which makes it easy to formulate exam questions based on the text.

If you've bought this book because "Of Mice and Men" is included in what you have to study for GCSE then, in my opinion, you've taken another step towards doing well in your exam.

<u>This guide has also been written specifically to assist GCSE candidates who are taking the OCR and AQA exams in Summer 2015.</u>

"Of Mice and Men" raises some timeless issues about how society (society in rural America in the 1930s, but also all societies, everywhere, at all times) treats the vulnerable and dispossessed. And, by getting to grips with this (and I can show you how), you'll have a head start to impressing the examiner.

But why a Gavin's Guide? It is likely you have browsed online or gone to a bookshop and discovered that there are numerous study guides on this text already. Many of them are useful reference points for summaries of the plot and the characters.

<u>Few, if any, explain or analyse in as much detail as this guide does how Steinbeck manages and organises our response as we read.</u>

It is understanding this – and being able to communicate you do to your examiner – that will mean you can achieve a good grade more easily.

I am a private tutor in Broadway, Worcestershire, and this book was initially written for my English Literature students. I wrote it to help them achieve good grades – and an understanding of what this clever, careful writer wanted to say. Now, in e-book form or paperback, I hope it may help you too.

What this short guide can do

This guide can help you to understand clearly what Steinbeck wanted to say when he wrote "Of Mice and Men".

It will also help you to improve your essay technique.

And you will discover what examiners like, and don't like, to see in your answers.

If you find watching worthwhile, as well as reading, I help you prepare to consider the values in the two film versions of the book. (Both the 1939 original and the more recent remake are widely available on DVD). I am aware that increasing numbers of teachers direct their pupils to watch these films, often in school lessons.

Putting into context what you see – because the exam will be based on the text alone, with no reference to these film versions – is crucial. Films of books inevitably have to leave a great deal out- and the 1939 film actually puts some of its own material in!

You can also email me direct – at grnsmithers@hotmail.co.uk- if you feel there is something that you still don't understand. I hope to help you further, or point you to further useful resources.

My love of literature began when I studied for an English degree at Oxford. Today, unravelling and appreciating language remains a lifelong passion. If this little book can move you towards that too – then it will be doubly worthwhile!

Interested? All you need is a few clear hours … and a willingness to begin with an open, curious mind.

This short, interpretative guide is intended as a supplement to, not a substitute for, teaching in a school.

It also comes with a big warning

…this guide will tell you what happens in the book right at the start.

I make no apologies for 'plot spoiling' – as it is quite deliberate. A Study Guide is useful

<u>after</u> you have read the novel – it is not a 'short-cut' that means you don't have to!

At GCSE level it is no longer enough to simply know what happened in a book. You need to look at the 'why' and 'how' of the way in which the writer has created his text.

Only by looking again at the structure of the story and seeing how it breaks down – sometimes as closely as word by word - can you gain a full understanding.

So! To recap. You should not read this guide until you have read the novel, *preferably twice*, **because I have written it in a way which demonstrates how the end of the story is in its beginning**.

Steinbeck's art and skill depend on links, connections and cross-references which we may not be consciously aware of, at first; I highlight these links.

If you read this study guide before you have read the novel, you will find the plot given away ahead of time- be warned!!

I believe that we must concentrate on developing a very clear sense of what the novel is about. The more we can define the meaning and message which lies behind the story, the greater our understanding and appreciation of Steinbeck's achievement will be.

What examiners want – and expressly __don't__ want too

Examiners' reports on the UK exam questions stress the need to be familiar with the text itself, and to build a sense of the characters and the meaning from that point. Every year, there are purely speculative comments made by less well prepared candidates, who may perhaps have had the novel read to them, when they need to have read it for themselves.

It is certainly true that Steinbeck has included everything we need to know about his characters' tendencies and temperaments. A close understanding of the text will give us more than enough to write about, without inventing more fictions of our own!

The other area examiners comment on is the forcing of material which does not belong there into an essay answer. Some of this material- typically, comments on some aspects of symbolism, themes and language- can be traced directly to particular revision guides. You can be reasonably sure that examiners will have read them too … and know that these comments are not your own independent thinking. Candidates can also misapply contextual/historical information about the "Dust Bowl", the Great Depression, and even the American Dream, when they import it into answers to essay questions which do not seek it.

There are also plenty of successful candidates, who can explain their personal response to the action and the characters, and who have interesting things to say about why Steinbeck does what he does; in other words, what his methods are. As with all literature study, being aware of how we ourselves feel, as we read, is the best guide we have to what the author is trying to do; it is unlikely that our emotional responses are random or accidental.

Steinbeck is very skilled at managing pace and dramatic tension; he makes time stand still, in the barn, after Lennie has killed Curley's wife, and then, at the end of the tale, the action is urgent; by taking the initiative, George deprives Curley of the grandstand finish he is hoping for. The killing of Lennie is as swift as the swallowing of the water snake by the heron.

This is not to say that there is no difference at all between how we read and respond and what Steinbeck seeks to evoke in us; after all, three quarters of a century, and its history, separates us from him. This is something I will return to later in this guide.

The secret to exam success

With any text, the key relationship is between the writer and the reader. Whether the writer simply wants to entertain or amuse us, or whether their aim is to prompt some serious thinking on our part about how the world works (or how it doesn't), they will have their own "voice", and their own methods.

In a novel, the story or narrative is told through what the characters do and what they say. In "Of Mice and Men", the main characters- Lennie, George, Curley's wife, Candy and Crooks- all convince as individuals, but they also stand for something larger than themselves- the plight of the vulnerable, the unskilled, the elderly, the ethnic minority. They become the means by which Steinbeck raises social issues.

In other words, Steinbeck is representing issues through the way he draws his characters and makes them behave. It is one of the features of the style of the novel that very little thinking goes on- these characters are not in the habit of reflecting!

The GCSE exam is designed to test how well you understand a writer's *methods* – or put more simply, how they manage to say what they say to us.

Characters use language as a method of communicating their thoughts and feelings to each other; writers use language (the language they give their characters) to communicate to us, the readers of the novel, the issues they want to provoke us into thinking about.

In this novel, we need to be able to explain what extra dimension each character brings to the overall meaning. So we need to be able to show how the characters' language affects and directs how we feel about them. For example, Curley's wife is spoken about very negatively before she makes her first appearance. That preconception (that she is a "tart") weakens as the narrative unfolds; we begin to see how frustrated and lonely she is; she alienates us when she bullies and threatens Crooks; but her death makes us more sympathetic again.

It is the difficulty of her situation, as the only woman on the ranch, and the boss's daughter-in-law, which prompts her bad behaviour, although it does not excuse it.

Steinbeck's characters speak in a way which betrays their lack of education, their suspicion of each other, and their emotional dysfunction. We look in vain- apart from in the friendship of George and Lennie- for much in the way of empathy or compassion.

The plot is very tightly constructed, to prepare us with a sense that Lennie's violent death is inevitable. It is clever of Steinbeck to arrange events so that George is absent and Lennie is alone with Curley's wife (just as he was alone with the unnamed girl in Weed).

The dream which has sustained George and Lennie through so many difficulties is within touching distance when it is taken cruelly from their grasp. And Carlson's Luger, associated so early with the shooting of Candy's hapless dog, has acquired layers of associated meaning before George takes it with him to "rescue" Lennie.

Nothing in the narrative is irrelevant. Everything has meaning. And yet the story works, just as a story, too. It is this technical skill and emotional power which make the novel so distinctive.

In your exam, you will be required to relate the content of a short extract to the narrative as a whole. This means that it is important for you to be able to see the story as continuous, and to thread together the experiences of the characters- like jewels strung together into a necklace.

The title and its relevance

Steinbeck originally intended his story to have the title "Something that happened"- a title which promises realism, but nothing more than the journalistic reporting of events.

The title "Of Mice and Men" comes from a poem by Robert Burns, who lived from 1759-1796, and whom we know best as the author of the words to the New Year song "Auld Lang Syne".

Steinbeck borrows his title from Burns' poem "To a Mouse", written in 1785, in which he says-

The best-laid schemes o' mice and men/ Gang aft a-gley/

And lea'e us nought but grief and pain/ For promised joy.

Or – as we might translate today:

"The best-laid plans of mice and men often go awry

And leave us nothing but grief and pain, for promised joy."

In the poem, the mouse is described as "cowering" and "timorous"; it feels "panic", and feels it has to run away.

Burns is reflecting on the fact that animals and people both experience their plan going wrong, so that, where we expect or hope for joy, we just feel grief and pain instead. Our best laid plans have as much chance of succeeding as a mouse's.

This choice of title- and the context of Burns' poem- puts the dream of the small farm right at the heart of Steinbeck's story. It promises joy to Lennie, to Candy, to Crooks (briefly) and to George. It comes tantalisingly close to becoming a reality, but the death of Curley's wife dashes it from their grasp, and dictates that Lennie dies too.

This is a graphic illustration of the cruel way our plans are thwarted, and, at the same time, it connects Lennie with the mouse. Lennie likes to pet mice (and, by killing them, accidentally, he ruins their plan, which is no more than to stay alive). Lennie's surname is Small; he is physically large, but his thinking ability is, perhaps, as small as a (small) mouse's.

The novel concludes with Lennie being in the same position as a mouse, trying to avoid being detected in the scrub near the pool, and suddenly being deprived of his own life. He has "petted" mice (and his puppy) to death, and, in the opening scene, George flung aside the corpse of the latest mouse; although Carlson took a shovel, in order to bury Candy's dog, there is no mention of a funeral for Lennie (perhaps because that would detract from the sense of shock).

Lennie feels the need to run away, when he and George are in the bunkhouse, and Curley's wife has just appeared for the first time; he feels the ranch is a mean place, and he is timorous or afraid. Later, when Curley physically attacks him, and when Curley's wife attacks Crooks verbally, both Lennie and Crooks are cowering; so, too, is Candy when his dog is shot.

These men, like mice, are exposed to sudden, extreme danger, grief and pain. Steinbeck wants to narrow the gap between the human race ("men") and the animal world ("mice") because he wants to expose how primitive life on the ranches is, and how the emotional orbit cannot extend to love because the need to survive- to kill or be killed- is so prominent.

Just as a mouse may face a violent end at any moment, workers on the ranch can be sacked or "canned" without notice; the few women who feature can be subjected to sudden, random sexual violence (in the cathouse, in Weed, or anywhere); and the few- like Curley- who have real power express it in an animalistic and brutal show of physical force.

Steinbeck: his life, his interests, his position as a writer

John Steinbeck was born in 1902. Even as a child, his own dream was only of being a writer; he pursued that ambition with remarkable persistence and determination. He died in 1968, after winning the Nobel Prize for Literature in 1962. In 1948, he had been elected to the American Academy of Letters.

His grandparents had been immigrants from Germany and Ireland, so the concept of the American Dream will have resonated with Steinbeck.

"Of Mice and Men" was his sixth novel, and his most successful to date, when it was published in 1937. A version of it for the stage won the Drama Critics' Circle Award. Steinbeck then won the Pulitzer Prize for fiction, and a place in the National Institute of Arts and Letters, as a result of the success of "The Grapes of Wrath", which appeared in 1939. Several of his novels have been made into feature films.

He wrote a novel which was successful in recruiting soldiers during the Second World War ("Bombs Away", 1942), and he advised on the Vietnam War. This public service element of his activities led to his award of the United States Medal of Freedom in 1964.

A cluster of his novels from the 1930s- not just "Of Mice and Men" and "The Grapes of Wrath", but also "Tortilla Flat" (1935) and "In Dubious Battle" (1936)- allow Steinbeck to concentrate on the plight of the migrant worker, who is easily exploited because he has no rights to a job, no real home and no security. As a student, he had worked on a ranch, bucking barley, and he also researched (and wrote non-fiction pieces about) the living conditions of unskilled workers in California.

He wrote to his publisher that his aim was "making people understand each other". We often see the characters in his novels failing to empathise when they meet someone whose way of life is different from theirs, whether the difference is social, economic, racial, or one of gender. In the world of the ranch, men and women regard each other with suspicion and emotional mistrust; the friendship of Lennie and George puzzles and disconcerts the boss and the other men. Steinbeck depicts a very mundane world, in which his characters find it difficult to tolerate or accept any form of difference. He says that his writing aims to show "the way lives are being lived". It is the way he manages realism and symbolism at the same time that distinguishes him from other novelists.

"The Grapes of Wrath" deals at much greater length with issues which are condensed in "Of Mice and Men"; without skills or education, families have no control over their destiny. They try to maintain their dignity and self-respect through working hard, and their motivation comes from their dream, which is to secure enough independence to give them relief from unremitting hard physical labour. Both novels shatter those dreams; in doing this, Steinbeck tells us that American society beats down the dream of the common man; the haves and the have-nots are fatally opposed, even in a land of plenty and supposed opportunity; and too much inequality will eventually lead to the dispossessed taking by force what they cannot gain through work. The pathos of the novels comes from the fact that the dreams are far from greedy, but still out of reach. The workers are modest, humble, conformist. But if those fortunate enough to have some wealth treat them callously, and exploit their labour, there will finally be a revolution.

In a letter, Steinbeck wrote that "Of Mice and Men" was "a tricky little thing designed to teach me to write for the theatre", and that he intended it to be "a study of the dreams and pleasures of everyone". This is not how it turned out; it may be that the theatrical dimension led the characters to take on the symbolic dimensions they have; for example, Crooks' embitterment, and his acute sense of the injustices he suffers, are not just personal to him- they encapsulate the wrongs done to so many people like him who were the innocent victims of deeply embedded racism.

Steinbeck set out his values as a writer in his acceptance speech for the Nobel Prize in 1962; the writer must "declare and celebrate man's proven capacity for greatness of heart and spirit- for gallantry in defeat, for courage, compassion and love". This could almost be a character sketch for George.

He also said, in that speech, that a serious writer should "passionately believe in the perfectibility of man". This suggests that he sees people as tending to be flawed or handicapped, but not condemned to remain so. The harshness of attitudes on the ranch is the consequence of hard lives, lived in a culture and society where caring for other people is beyond the capability of those whose ambition is just to keep working, in order not to be homeless.

While the narrative gives very little hope that anything can, or will, improve in the way people treat each other on the ranches of California, George has already learned about his own "perfectibility", in that Lennie's complete trust in following his instructions- even at the risk of drowning-has led George to behave less cruelly, and more compassionately, towards him. Instead of taking advantage of Lennie, because he was too dumb to take care of himself, and making himself seem smarter (to himself) than he really is, George decided to concentrate on keeping Lennie physically safe (which, ironically, he proves unable to do).

The impossible choices George has to make at the end of the narrative- to kill Lennie himself, and face the fact that there will now be nothing to distinguish him from the other labourers, so that, stripped of his dream, he, too, will spend all he has earned at the end of the month, and blot out thoughts of the future- do constitute "gallantry in defeat".

Steinbeck's argument is that, though there are good men and bad men, there is still an essential dignity in making your living through physical labour. What makes the work itself less dignified is that the crops and the fields are owned by someone else, who profits excessively and disproportionately from that labour.

"Meanness" is the by-product of a society which treats its working classes meanly.

The Nobel Prize speech did not shy away from the writer's duty to examine the less attractive aspects of humanity; Steinbeck says that "the writer.....is charged with exposing our many grievous faults and failures, with dredging up to the light our dark and dangerous dreams for the purpose of improvement".

He certainly dredges up the dark and dangerous nature of life on the ranch, and leaves us with a clear understanding that the passing of this way of life does open up the way to "improvement"- but only if the lessons of Lennie's death are learned. The animalistic and primitive ethos of the ranch is close to Nature only really in the sense that it is subhuman. A humane society would not put Lennie to death.

Commentary on the text

The novel is in six sections, or scenes; each of the first five is longer than we would expect a chapter of a novel to be today. The book was made into a play soon after it was published, and you can imagine how the settings or backdrops of each of the six sections could be managed comfortably in the theatre.

The sixth and final scene is deliberately short. The narrative ends with a gunshot, and like a gunshot; there is a sudden loud noise, and then a shocked silence, after which there is nothing left to say.

The story will come full circle; in the time from when George and Lennie arrive, on a Thursday evening, to the time when Lennie is killed, on the following Sunday, they start work at the ranch, witness the shooting of Candy's dog, and encounter the same kind of trouble which had forced them to come here from Weed in the first place- Lennie's disastrous habit of not letting go of soft things which he likes to "pet".

Section One

The sense that the end of the novel is a true ending comes from two things- the technique of "foreshadowing" which Steinbeck uses, to prepare us for the events to come, by hinting at them beforehand; and through the careful description of the landscape.

 The setting right at the start of the novel has a mood and colour all of its own. The action takes place to the south of Soledad. We are told (as well as being able to imagine from the pure sound of the word) that this place name means "loneliness".

So! Now let's take a close look at the first two paragraphs. Colours, sounds and animals provide the detail. The river is described as being deep, and its colour green; the willow trees are the same colour –green- and the fact that they are so fresh each Spring is also noted; look too at how colour is also used to describe the sycamore trees, the foothills of the Gabilan mountains and even the rabbits. The sands and the pool are also given colours, respectively yellow, and green.

The leaves which have fallen from the trees lie "deep and…crisp"; if a lizard runs through them, there will be "a great skittering". The rabbits are very quiet. When they come out of an evening they make no noise; they sit on the sand banks in silence – and check the text here for a truly beautiful description of the heron that appears. The scene-setting concludes with footsteps scrunching on leaves, as the yet to be identified George and Lennie walk down the track from the highway.

This scene is full of sunlight and happy expectation. It is evening on a hot day. The water is warm, and boys from the ranches come here to swim. The rabbits come out in the evening, when it is cooler. The sense we have is of a place where animals abound, but are easily frightened. The sycamore trees are personified- their branches are described as having recumbent limbs, and a sycamore branch or trunk acts as seating for the men who make camp fires here.

It is important that we know this place well, as it has significance in the plot. This is the place of safety which George will tell Lennie to come to if he gets into trouble; when Lennie obeys the instruction, after accidentally killing Curley's wife, the sense of safety is ironic, because George is coming, not to rescue Lennie, but to kill him.

The matching description in the first four paragraphs of section six sets the scene for Lennie's killing. Look at it and you will be able to pick out the phrases that resonate with what you have just read at the start of the book. Look in particular at how Steinbeck describes the pool, the time of day, the sun and the hilltops.

There is a heron standing in the pool this time around. Inventively, a little water snake acts in the same innocent and unconcerned way as the lizard did in scene one.

But, this time, the heron is a predator; it catches and swallows the helpless little water snake, with a sudden movement. This time, it does not fly away; it stands "motionless and waiting". When another water snake appears, we expect it, too, to be killed; but then Lennie arrives, and although he comes quietly, he, and the breeze, disturb the heron, which pounds the air with its wings, and flies down river.

At a stroke, by repeating these details, Steinbeck makes us feel that this is a familiar place (just as Lennie does), and he has introduced a sense of foreboding through the killing of the helpless water snake. Lennie is just as helpless and "little", in the sense that a deadly act of violence is about to be done to him.

The remainder of scene one introduces us to George and Lennie, and establishes the nature of their relationship and the events which have brought them here.

George is small and quick, with restless, red-rimmed eyes; he is wary and cautious, from constantly having to watch out for any trouble Lennie may get into. There are flashes of tenderness in his attitude to Lennie, and flashes of frustration, or even anger, too.

He points out to Lennie that, if he were autonomous, he would have a life with what he describe as no mess at all; he could live easily, because he would have no trouble in his life- being run out of Weed is not the first time Lennie's behaviour has lost them their jobs.

George particularly misses the freedom of being able to go into town and get whatever he wants. This proves ironic, because it is on the one occasion George does this that Lennie is left alone with Curley's wife, with doubly fatal consequences.

There is more dramatic irony when George points out to Lennie that he cannot live independently, and that somebody would shoot him, mistaking him almost for vermin if he was by himself, just lurking around on the edge of town. He does not know that the person who shoots Lennie will eventually be him, to prevent it from being Curley.

Later, in Section Three, George sets out the case again for a life with no mess; it involves a whorehouse with a fixed price menu for drinks and sexual services. So his needs are base and basic. But he also has a loftier vision of what might make for a better, more meaningful life; and so he has hit on the alternative plan to save for the farm, rather than blowing his wages on drink and women. The dream or plan is real enough, to begin with, but it has the extra advantage of being a means of captivating, distracting and controlling Lennie, just like a baby's favourite soft toy.

It is this plan which serves to prove to himself that he is smarter than his colleagues. As he explains it to Slim, if he were bright, or even just slightly smart, he would have found a way to own his own smallholding by now; but, as Crooks and Curley's wife both point out, if it were that simple, someone would have done it by now- and no-one has, because it is the impossible dream. No man can keep their eyes on the prize for long enough, because it is too far away, and the frustrations and boredom of labouring life always get in the way.

Lennie is described as a huge man with wide, sloping shoulders, and arms which hang loosely at his sides; the impression is that he is uncoordinated. Where George has sharp and strong features, Lennie's face is like his mind- it is shapeless, with large, pale eyes. He is not dynamic; his feet drag. He is not paying attention, so that, when George stops in the clearing, Lennie almost walks into him. We realise that all the thinking and planning (even for something as mundane as how to walk along a road) has to be done on his behalf.

Lennie admires George, and he expresses that in trying to copy his movements, looking over at him, copying what gestures he can.

It is very clear that Lennie has a bad memory, despite his best efforts to remember what he is told; he has forgotten where they are going; forgotten that George has his work card; forgotten, superficially, what had happened in Weed; forgotten precisely who his Aunt Clara was; and he says that he cannot remember all the elements of the often-recited dream about the rabbits which George has told him so often- although, where this is concerned, sometimes he seems to forget on purpose.

When George entrusts to him the task of gathering wood for the fire, Lennie goes across the river to find a mouse instead. His attention span is very short. He can barely feed himself without making a mess. He gets George to tell him the story of their "dream" (of owning and farming their own piece of land) as a comforting bedtime story- again, it is supremely ironic that this hypnotic mantra will be the last thing Lennie hears before George shoots him. He falls asleep thinking of furry rabbits of different colours.

The same childish unworldliness applies to the glee with which Lennie throws himself at the water in the pool. George is cautious and nervous about it, because it seems to be stagnant. But Lennie has already played with it (and there is a great evocative description of this in the book). Lennie had been sick the night before- presumably from drinking too much dirty water- but his enthusiasm wipes his memory clear.

Just as every part of George is "defined", while Lennie is "shapeless", George has all the native caution, and Lennie, like a small child just starting to walk, has none. Later, by ignoring or forgetting George's warnings that he must stay away from Curley's wife, Lennie sets off the catastrophic final episode.

Rather than go straight to the new ranch, after a four-mile walk, George decides that they will stay overnight in the clearing. He knows that the work on the ranch will be physically hard. In fact, the decision is Steinbeck's (not George's!), and it creates a space in which he can dramatise, through the dialogue, the background information that creates the context for the narrative which will start when they report for work at the ranch. Once the setting has moved there, there is little time or space to give the reader a back story. All of the essential scene-setting has to be done here, by the pool.

One of the key successes of this opening section is the way in which Steinbeck makes us appreciate how difficult it is to look after Lennie, and how much pressure George is always under. We understand this from George's tone of voice, and from the adverbs which describe him. He stares morosely and speaks sharply, angrily, disgustedly, furiously. It takes a varied arsenal of adverbs to reflect the full range of the emotional pressure he suffers! Small wonder that, when Lennie wishes they had ketchup to put on the beans, George finally loses patience and snaps at him.

What frustrates George is not just the fact that, wherever they go, Lennie gets them into trouble. He cannot go out, cannot have a social life with his co-workers, playing pool; he cannot drink (whisky). He is always on duty, looking out for Lennie.

In his more private dreams, he wonders whether, without Lennie, he could maybe meet a girl and have a partner (although, from what we see later of life on the ranch, and its almost zero number of women this seems unlikely). While none of the other characters (except for Slim, right at the very end) empathises with George over his burden of care, the reader does empathise with him, very much, and from the beginning. When the time comes, it would be very harsh to judge that George was wrong to have the couple of hours away which leave Lennie unattended, and leave Curley's wife and Lennie in such unexpected danger.

Lennie's emotions are simple and transparent. He cries like a baby; his lip quivers, when George is angry. He alternately backs away, or comes closer to George, depending on whether he feels disapproved of or not. When he drinks water, the simple pleasure of it is enough to ensure that he is happy and smiling. He looks at George timidly when he senses he has displeased him.

The occasional power of a good memory recalled, or a happy thought, means that Lennie will smile at once, or giggle, unaware of what other people may think this means. He keeps nothing back, and has no mental capacity to think he ever should. So, when he realises he has forgotten what he has been told, he is startled or puzzled (not embarrassed, which is a more complex emotion). Curley attacks him because he misreads Lennie's thoughts (which are of rabbits, and the dream).

The strain of thinking shows on his face, which becomes tight with the effort of it. When he realises he has not lost his work card, he grins with relief; when he is disappointed, he hangs his head.

When he senses that George is angry with him, his face becomes drawn with terror, no less; and he is truly (if briefly) anguished. When George recites the fairy tale of their dream, he is delighted, and when George praises him for remembering the simplest instruction, he is overcome with pride, because he is unable to do half-measures. It is all wonderful or all disaster with him.

How he reacts to his dream about the rabbits is also interesting. He becomes so excited at the recitation of the dream that he interrupts, laughs and shouts with delight. Nothing else animates him so much, and he falls asleep thinking of imaginary rabbits. This preoccupation with the world of the unreal and the imagination is one of the things which make Lennie less of a man and more of a child.

Another is his knowledge of how he can manipulate George, by pretending to be capable of being more independent than he is, and exploiting George's sense of duty, protectiveness and affection- something which, when we become parents, we may allow our "small" children to do to us from time to time!

Lennie's physical movements are equally unsophisticated, like those of an overgrown toddler. He lumbers to his feet and crashes around. He has not learned to use body language effectively- he may pretend innocence when he doesn't want to be found out (perhaps when he has forgotten to do something) but George always knows when Lennie is hiding something from him.

It is interesting that, when George forces him to hand over the dead mouse, Lennie comes to him slowly, like a dog who doesn't want to bring a ball to its master but does so, finally, because it knows it has no choice but to obey. Candy's dog is reliant on Candy because it is a dog; Lennie is reliant on George because he is not capable of surviving on his own.

The canine imagery extends to when George throws the mouse into the scrub. Lennie then lets out a whimpering cry and, a few lines later, he looked as a dog would look sadly up at his owner when it was doing something it would prefer not to, but has been trained to do, such as coming back when called. Thinking of Lennie as George's pet dog adds an extra layer of poignancy to the parallel between his shooting and the shooting of Candy's dog in Section Three.

Lennie does, though, possess a sort of animal cunning, which we see at first hand towards the end of this opening scene. George's frustration has got the better of him, and he vocalises what he would never normally say- that, without Lennie, he would have a great time, an easier life.

Almost as soon as he has said it, George feels ashamed and mean for saying these things out loud, because Lennie cannot help being as he is, and his sense of guilt leads him to tell Lennie three times that he wants them to stay together; he also promises to get him a puppy at the first opportunity, in the hope that a bigger animal than a mouse, when Lennie strokes it, will not die (events later on will prove that this is a vain and ironic hope too).

Lennie has few variations of speech style, but he can still recognise that George's feelings of guilt have given him the upper hand, for the moment. In an early example of a number of fishing images at intervals throughout the novel, he avoids the bait (later, he cannot resist the "bait" of Curley's wife).

Our experience when we read this opening scene is rather like George's; we know how often Lennie has got into trouble before, but we hope that his apparently redoubled effort now to avoid the same mistakes will succeed, at least for long enough to enable them to save enough to buy their farm.

We are looking for the triumph of hope over experience; it fails to happen, more often than not. George's contingency plan for what Lennie must do will when their best laid plans go wrong will, of course, be needed. But George pins his hopes on the threat that, if Lennie gets into trouble again, he won't let him look after rabbits. Ironically, of course, Lennie does-very soon- get into even worse trouble than ever before; and the result is that there will never be any rabbits for anyone to tend.

Moreover, George knows how limited Lennie's capacity is; he had promised to let Lennie light the fire, but he does it himself; and he refers to Lennie, both affectionately and critically, as a crazy bastard (three times), then a fool, a son of a bitch, but always with the 'affectionate' qualifier of 'crazy'.

The opening scene ends with more dogs and more personification of the sycamores. We know, somehow, that the animal and the human are coexisting here in a way which is not exactly civilised and not exactly safe. George belongs to the world of work, the adult and human world; Lennie is oddly at home in the outdoors.

In his natural habitat of the present moment-
with his lack of memory, and his inability to
anticipate the future- he is really like a dog
or a water snake or a horse or a bear.
Trying to bring the animal that is Lennie into
the world of people feels uncomfortable,
and it feels dangerous.

SectionTwo

The second scene takes place in the bunkhouse on the ranch, and it introduces all of the main characters except Crooks- Candy, then the boss, then Curley, Curley's wife, Slim, Carlson, and Candy's dog.

The atmosphere is hot and claustrophobic. Curley's unprovoked aggression indicates that there may be trouble ahead; both Lennie and George feel uncomfortable about him, and George is anxious that Curley's wife may be a magnet for Lennie, because of her softness and her preference for wearing red.

George's plan becomes clear. They need to stay for a month, to build up a sum of $100; in order to do that, they will need to avoid trouble of any sort. Then they can go prospecting for gold, which might earn them a couple of dollars a day, plus extra if they find gold (presumably still in California). Candy's hints that Curley is in the habit of picking physical fights with men who are bigger than him puts Lennie in a particularly dangerous and vulnerable position.

Reading the scene, we understand that the issue is precisely as George had presented it to us in the clearing the night before. Lennie's capacity for getting into trouble, and losing them their jobs, will be tested by both Curley and Curley's wife. Lennie cannot even adhere to the carefully reiterated instruction that he should say nothing at all when they meet the boss; and his strategy of trying to say nothing at all to Curley seems just to antagonise him even more.

There are hints that Slim will be sympathetic to George, and to his compassion for, and friendship with, Lennie. The fact that Slim has a dog which has just had five puppies makes it possible that Lennie may be able to take care of one, and thus avoid other kinds of trouble. Once again, there is irony here- if Lennie did not have the puppy, he would not be in the barn, and his conversation with Curley's wife, alone, would not have taken place.

George lies four times in this scene. He tells the boss that they have had to walk ten miles to the ranch that morning; that they left Weed because their work there was over; that Lennie is George's cousin; and that Lennie was kicked in the head by a horse as a young child. It is not clear at this point why he should be so desperate to be taken on at the ranch; later, as we find out how close he is to striking a deal to purchase the small farm, that will make Lennie's dream a reality, and be their escape from a life of servility, we look back and understand his motive.

The broader context is that these jobs, through Murray and Ready, are under Roosevelt's "New Deal" that helped people like Lennie and George find work; there may not be many other jobs at many other ranches to go to.

It is one of Steinbeck's apt brushstrokes that the job George says they were doing in Weed was digging a cesspool. In a figurative sense, if not a literal one, they were.....and the same thing will happen on this ranch. (We are given no explanation of how George and Lennie met the girls in Weed, one of whom cried for help because she felt Lennie was trying to assault her).

The bunkhouse has one door, and it is sparely furnished, with eight beds, each of which has an apple box above it for its occupant's belongings. Three of the beds are vacant; that is why George and Lennie have been sent here to work.

The only leisure pursuit is a pack of cards, and the ranch men have Western magazines which they laugh at but actually privately believe, presumably because they contain tales of heroism and love, and look back to the cowboy age (of freedom) which has given way to the age of captive cheap labouring.

The sun is shining through one of the windows, and the beam of light highlights the flies. Flies are unavoidable on ranches, because there are horses there; but flies are also a symbol of death and decay. Later in this scene, they are described as sparks. Sparks are emblematic of fire, conflict, danger and damage.

As Candy introduces George and Lennie to the bunkhouse, Lennie is, once again, the follower, and George the leader. Candy has lost his right hand.

George is suspicious of the reasons why the previous occupant of the bed Candy offers him- a blacksmith called Whitey- left the ranch. Candy says he complained about the food, but in the end there is no certain explanation for why anyone leaves- the lack of the sense of belonging, the rootlessness of this way of life, means that asking for an explanation is unnecessary.

George does not believe Candy's explanation, and he is slowly getting angry, but keeping it under wraps for now. Lennie does not imitate him in this, but he does in the ritual of making his bed (just as he had been copying George's gestures and postures the night before).

The boss arrives, as Candy finishes explaining that he provided whisky for the white ranch-hands at Christmas, and practises/condones discrimination against his one coloured employee, Crooks. According to Candy, Crooks is nice, and so too is the boss and Slim, all to differing degrees. But using the same word to describe how he feels about all three points to another meaning – that Candy has a pathological fear of upsetting anyone. This is no doubt because his employment is precarious, as it will not be long until he himself is of no practical use on this ranch or indeed any other.

Steinbeck introduces the boss, as he does all his characters, with a detailed description of his clothing and build. The boss wears high-heeled boots and spurs to show he is not a worker; this seems unnecessary, as everyone on the ranch knows who he is anyhow.

Steinbeck's point is that those who do not work have to find ways of validating themselves; the dignity and value of the worker is one of the motivators of Steinbeck's novels, particularly his great, long novel about displacement, "The Grapes of Wrath".

The boss tries to make Lennie speak for himself, and suspects that George is exploiting Lennie, and taking his pay, because he has never seen any man look out for another less able man before; the concept of friendship or mutual concern is alien to the culture of the ranch. He remains unconvinced, and tells George he will keep his eye on him.

George accuses Lennie of almost losing them the work, through speaking up- although all Lennie did was to repeat, with a smile, George's description of him as being strong. George wants Lennie to say nothing to anyone, because he could so easily slip up and say the wrong thing.

Candy's dog appears, with Candy. It is old, pale and wizened like Candy. Its movement is a lame struggle (Candy shuffles). George suspects that Candy, who is bored, underemployed and nosey, has been eavesdropping. Candy's defence is that, on the ranch, you neither listen nor ask any questions- you stay away from any possible involvement with other people. Candy's isolation, by virtue of his uselessness, causes him an acute lack of status, and extreme insecurity and anxiety; he will be disposed of, when he can no longer do anything useful, just as his dog will be, in the next section of the narrative.

Before Candy can recite a detailed biography of his dog, Curley appears; thin, with a brown face, brown eyes, curly hair, and a work glove on his left hand. He, too, is wearing high-heeled boots. His constant appearances, demanding to know where his father (or his wife) is, are a means of asserting himself, demanding to be noticed; and they show that he has nothing worthwhile to do.

His wife, too, will be driven, through loneliness and neglect, to do the same; though we come to understand later that she is merely seeking company and human contact. Ironically for her, the power she has, of being attractive to the men, is of no benefit to her, because they are all too scared (that the pathologically jealous and controlling Curley may have them sacked) to engage in conversation with her; the exception is Slim, who seems neither afraid of Curley, nor intimidated by her looks.

Curley's body language gives him away; he is as simple in his instincts as Lennie. He looks coldly at George and Lennie, and he involuntarily moves into a boxer's stance.

In response to Curley's demands, Lennie makes a harmless comment ("We jus' come in"), which gives Curley a sense of power; Candy explains Curley's experience as a lightweight boxer who was always able and eager to take on bigger guys. George prophetically predicts- foreshadowing the crushing of Curley's hand- that there will be trouble, and that Curley will suffer at Lennie's hands.

Even Candy, who has a weak sense of morality, sees that Curley picks his fights in a way which is unfair. He points out, too, that, because it is his father's ranch, Curley has an unfair advantage which allows him to be as aggressive and bullying as he likes; moreover, he seems to have become worse since he was married a fortnight earlier (sexual jealousy of his wife makes him even more edgy and aggressive).

Candy amplifies the sense we are getting that this is the worst possible time for George and Lennie to arrive at the ranch, when he goes on to talk about Curley's wife; she is pretty, and, he says, flirtatious to the point of seduction.

At this point, we do not know how reliable Candy is; he says that she is a tart, but he is old, gossipy, and, if he is as much like his dog as his dog is like him, half-blind.

George (usefully) warns Lennie that Curley thinks he has scared him, and that he will try to follow this up with a physical attack. He knows that if Lennie fights back they will both be thrown off the ranch, because he's the boss's son, and he suggests that Lennie simply refuses to engage with him.

Importantly, though- fatally so- George is not prepared to let Curley victimise Lennie, so his final instruction is to fight back if the other man hits out first. Curley is such a caveman- so unevolved- that matching violence with violence is the only effective way to deal with him.

Next- and ironically- Curley's wife appears in the doorway, artfully framed against the sun. She is fatal to George and Lennie's optimistic hopes of escaping this way of life. Her voice is unattractive in a harsh, nasal way, but she is dressed to show off, and attract male attention; fully made up, and accessorised, with red fingernails, and red mules on her feet. She dresses as if she has just been on a theatre cabaret or film set, which, we learn later, is precisely where she dreams of being.

She claims to be looking for Curley, but it is more likely that she has heard (from him or his father) that two new men have arrived, and she has come to see for herself.

She stands provocatively and smiles. She tries to encourage George, by saying it is fine to look at her, because everyone can look where they will, whatever their status. But George is not interested in her. Lennie cannot helping looking at her (because she is dressed in red, like the girl in Weed), but she doesn't like this, as he isn't looking at her in a sexual, appreciative way, which is what she wants. When Slim alerts her to the fact that Curley may not be far away, she hurries off.

Her flirtatiousness is opportunistic; but, as we come to appreciate later, her loneliness is continual. In the light of what she says in section Four and section Five, about not liking her husband and being a little afraid, it is quite possible that she is trying to avoid him, rather than afraid that he will catch her talking to the men.

Lennie is hopelessly impressed; he smiles at her prettiness. George is uncompromising; he shakes Lennie by the ear, and tells him not to even look at her! This is ironic; George can envisage a repeat of the alleged sexual incident in Weed, because Lennie's instincts are so simple, and his memory and ability to learn from his experiences so impaired, but he does not imagine that Lennie might kill her.

The urgency of George's warnings (and he tweaks his ear in case words aren't enough) elicits genuine fear in Lennie, who wants them to leave, but George tells him they must stay until they have earned some money. This conversation is conveniently cut short by the arrival of Slim. Steinbeck's description of him is unusual-because he tells us that he is so majestic looking that other people stop what they are doing to take his word on any subject, from politics to love.

There is a famous maxim that any aspiring novelist should "show, not tell", so it is surprising when one as skilful as Steinbeck breaks that very useful convention. The likeliest explanation is that, in a short novel which has no time for scenes set in the fields, Steinbeck wants to establish Slim's authority quickly and unambiguously.

More convincing than the rather breathless and uncritical admiration with which Steinbeck describes him is the fact that Slim is the only character who is unafraid. George fears Lennie's "messes".

By contrast, see how the other characters react. Thus Lennie fears George's displeasure, and the power George has to bar him from feeding the future rabbits; Candy fears being sacked, and old age;

Curley fears being outfought; Crooks fears Curley's wife's power to have him hanged on invented charges of attempted rape; Curley's wife fears her loneliness and the consequences of her mistake in marrying Curley.

Slim speaks gently to George; he is friendly; he readily accepts the basis of the friendship between George and Lennie, and says he doesn't know why more people don't have same sex friends. At the very end of the novel, Slim's instinctive empathy for George, and his understanding of the moral dilemma he faced, holds out the possibility that he and George might now form a lasting friendship.

George's explanation of his arrangement with Lennie – that they look after one another - refers back to the previous scene, when it was also mentioned, but not understood by everyone else.

Quite how Lennie looks after George is unclear, except that the feeling of responsibility George derives from caring for Lennie brings its own satisfaction. It seems to allay loneliness; but we are already aware of the complications this has brought with it.

Carlson appears; he is a powerful man with a big stomach who makes a weak joke, twice, about Lennie not being "small". The way he repeats it suggests he is not very quick-witted. He moves on to the subject of Slim's dog and the litter it has just had. Slim has already, unsentimentally, drowned four of the nine puppies, and kept the larger ones- an effective example of the culture of the survival of the fittest, or Darwin's natural selection, on the ranch. Is it too fanciful to see in this number- four drowned- the foreshadowing of the arithmetic of death in the novel; the deaths of two more dogs (Candy's, and Lennie's puppy) and two humans/dogs (Curley's wife and Lennie)?

Carlson suggests that Candy could have one of the puppies, and that they could persuade him to shoot his old dog, which smells bad, can see little, and cannot eat solid food. The analogy with elderly people is clear, and chilling. Those who are old, and incapable of fending for themselves, can (and should, in Carlson's view) be disposed of, to make room for the next generation.

The fate of Candy's dog is left undecided, and Lennie's misgivings about staying (and being a potential target for Curley) are drowned out by his hope that Slim may have a puppy he can have.

The scene ends with Curley reappearing, looking for his wife. He looks at George more closely, and sees that he is much the same shape and size as him, and therefore not a target for a fight.

As the bunkhouse empties, Candy's old dog comes back. This time, it does not even have the energy to walk about, or search for Candy. It is unaware of what will be done to it, just as Lennie is unaware of what will happen to him. Unlike the dog which answered the coyote in the last sentence of the first scene, Candy's dog has no voice in the last sentence of this second one.

Section Three

The next scene takes place that same Friday evening, in the bunkhouse. George and Lennie have done their first shift in the fields. Slim has given one of the remaining puppies to Lennie. He admires the physical strength Lennie has shown in his work. George, ironically, asserts that Lennie can take orders; but as we know, the order to keep out of trouble is always too complicated for him to manage.

Slim picks up the thread of his earlier conversation with George, about the nature of his relationship with Lennie. George explains that he knew Lennie's Aunt Clara because he was born in the same town as Lennie. When Aunt Clara died, they started to work together. George says that he used to play practical jokes on Lennie, but he never retaliated. George felt smart in comparison, but he dropped his inconsiderateness, cruelty and exploitation after he put Lennie in danger of drowning.

George has no family, and he sees Lennie as his insurance against being endlessly alone and lonely. We hear fully what actually happened in Weed; how Lennie, who simply wants to touch everything he likes, and is mesmerised by the colour red, touched a girl's red dress. When the girl screamed, he became confused and scared and just held on, until George rescued him by hitting him on the head with a fence post.

The girl made an allegation of rape against Lennie (although there was no sexual or aggressive motive on Lennie's part), and a lynch party set out to capture him, but they hid under water in a ditch and escaped.

The detail in this account is important, because it is filed in the reader's memory. When we reach the point where Lennie and Curley's wife are in the barn, we realise long before it happens what the sequence of events will be; only, this time, Lennie will feel he must find a way to stop the girl from screaming, because if he does not, George will not let him tend the rabbits; fear of the consequences of an action (Curley's wife screaming) leads to a far worse action (breaking her neck, by accident).

Lennie's essential harmlessness (apart from his physical strength) is emphasised, first through Slim's repeated judgment that Lennie is nice and not mean – and that he, Slim, is a good judge of who is or isn't mean; and, secondly, through Lennie's breathless infatuation with his brown and white puppy, which he tries to smuggle into the bunkhouse. Slim can see that Lennie has a child's simple-mindedness; all he wants to do is to pet the puppy.

George sends Lennie back out to the barn with his puppy, which needs to be with its mother to feed; his ruse of lying on his bunk and turning his face to the wall is obvious to George, who is expert at telling when Lennie is holding on to small creatures, dead or alive (like the mouse in the opening scene).

After Lennie has gone, Candy comes in with his dog. Candy is suffering with an upset stomach, from eating turnips. Carlson arrives, and tells Candy that his dog smells so bad that he must take it outside. He asserts that the dog is no good to Candy and asks Candy why he doesn't shoot the dog. Candy's explanation is that he has had the dog all its life (an exact reflection of the relationship between George and Lennie) and that the dog had been a brilliant sheep dog. Slim has said much the same about Lennie, when he said he'd never seen anyone work with such strength.

Carlson insists that shooting the dog can be done humanely, with a bullet in the back of the head; when Candy resists, out of loyalty and sentimentality, Carlson offers to shoot the dog himself, and accuses Candy of being unkind to the dog by keeping it alive.

Slim sides with Carlson, in the argument that what is old and useless should be put out of its misery- in fact, it is what he would want for himself. This is laced with irony, because Candy himself is only one step removed from being described like that.

Steinbeck builds the dramatic tension in the scene by using a short diversion, where the young labourer Whit shows Slim and George a letter in a magazine written by one of their former co-workers.

But Carlson returns remorselessly to the issue of the dog. Each of Candy's objections- that the smell isn't so bad; that he is loyal to the dog, its lifetime companion; that it might suffer, if shot; that he should kill his dog himself; that there is no gun; that they should wait till tomorrow- is ignored. Slim's refusal to let the dog live reduces Candy to a hopeless consent, even though it is the last thing that he really wants to do.

Carlson speaks to the dog with a gentleness which belies his intentions, and the dog obediently follows him outside. Slim reminds Carlson to take a shovel, so that he buries the dog immediately.

This episode foreshadows or prefigures events later on. Lennie will be shot, like Candy's dog, in the back of the head, with Carlson's gun, after his fate has been decided by Slim, who discounts any other options when he speaks to George in the barn; the world of the ranch sees it as a mercy killing, but we find it unnatural and uncivilised, and the lack of compassion disturbs us. Once the dog cannot keep itself clean, Candy's attachment to it counts for nothing.

Candy, who is responsible for the dog, has no say in the decision about the killing, or the timing of it. Carlson simply says that it may as well happen right away. The decision is made by Slim, and the principle behind it is that the old and immobile should be shot. Lennie's shooting is worse, because he is neither old nor useless, but he, too, in accidentally killing Curley's wife, has left a (metaphorical) smell so bad that it cannot be ignored.

It is painful for the reader to experience how Candy has no right to be heard, or to decide the fate of his own dog. George will find himself in the same position when Slim decides that it is more humane to shoot Lennie, in precisely this way, than to let him face the full force of Curley's bloodthirsty desire for revenge, or commit him to a life in captivity.

We will also see that Crooks' apparent rights and control over his own life are equally fragile, when Curley's wife takes out her frustration on him and threatens to have him hanged. There is a latent threat of violence all the time, with Curley; but the whole way of life on the ranch is one where killing is the accepted answer to a social problem. There is no question of caring for, understanding, or rehabilitating the old, the infirm or the damaged.

Steinbeck puts some weak lines of attempted conversation into the mouths of George and Slim, but the emphasis is on the silence, as everyone waits to hear the gunshot. The same ominous state of paralysis hangs over the barn, when Curley's wife is dead but undiscovered.

Candy has been staring at the ceiling, in a state of resigned despair, still and rigid, while the others talk. Once the shot is heard, he faces the wall, still silent. We can imagine his grief and his sense of shame at being overruled, and unable to save the dog.

Over a card game with George, Whit revives the idea that Curley's wife is deliberately provocative. George uses the word mess to predict what will happen. This turn of phrase reminds us that, in the opening scene, he said that, without Lennie, he would have no mess to deal with.

Whit explains to George what their Saturday night in the town involves, and which of the two brothels they prefer, and why; he invites George to go with them, but George explains that he is saving his money, but may join them for a drink.

This is important to the plot, because it creates the circumstances in which Lennie finds himself alone with Crooks, and then in a discussion with Candy and Curley's wife, later on. In that conversation, her warmth towards Lennie paves the way for their fateful encounter in the barn the following afternoon.

Carlson cleans his gun. Lennie has returned, furtively, because he has a secret on his mind. Whit and Carlson go outside because they think Curley means to pick a fight with Slim. George tries to remind Lennie of the danger Curley's wife represents, but Lennie interrupts him; he has accidentally killed his puppy, but George is unaware of that, and Lennie wants to know when they will be able to buy the farm.

When George points out to Lennie that they do not yet have enough money, Candy suddenly pays attention, as does Lennie, as George describes the ten acre smallholding and the way they could live there. This is not just the dream he has recited so often, and in the opening scene; it is a more defined, specific, concrete and tangible version of it.

It represents an easier life- six or seven hours' work a day, instead of eleven hours of hard labour, and the capacity to sell their own produce. George will make things there resemble his memories of his own childhood, and his grandfather's piggery. Most importantly, they will be independent. While his own version of the future is more hard-edged than Lennie's- it involves killing rabbits and chickens for food- he has thought about it in great detail, and becomes engrossed with imagining how good it will be.

George tells Candy that the farm will cost $600 to buy; Candy already has $300 ($250 compensation for losing his hand four years ago- five months' pay) with a further $50 due in ten or eleven days' time, at the end of the month. George and Lennie only have $10, but he thinks that if they stay for a month and earn $100, that might be enough. George could earn the balance later while Lennie and Candy started on the farm.

Suddenly, the dream is capable of being made real. Candy explains that soon he will no longer be able to clean the bunkhouse, and then he will lose his job.

Candy's future is as bleak as his dog's had been, and George and Lennie's dream offers him, too, the security a primitive welfare system cannot. The completely unexpected closeness, now, to making their plans come true is a source of child-like joy. Steinbeck shows just how good it is by using the words "beauty" and "lovely". Common enough words generally, but they have not been used in this novel before.

Slim, Curley, Whit and Carlson reappear. Curley has accused Slim of taking too much interest in his wife, and is having to apologise, when Slim stands up to him. Now it is Carlson's turn to say something prophetic – he tells Curley that if his wife keeps hanging around the bunkhouse, then there is bound to be trouble; and it won't be the men's fault. Curley is meeting unaccustomed resistance to his bullying, which only makes his determination to pick an easy fight even stronger.

Next, there is a misunderstanding. Lennie is having a happy smile about the dream of the farm and the rabbits, but Curley thinks he is laughing at him, and attacks him, punching him in the face three times.

There is no retaliation, because Lennie is too frightened to defend himself. As Curley continues his assault, George restrains Slim and tells Lennie to hit back. It is only after the third instruction, with his face covered in blood, that Lennie responds.

He catches Curley's flying fist. Just as in Weed, Lennie, frightened, does not let go;

George hits him (as he did in Weed) but Lennie does not let go, until George has shouted at him repeatedly (just as he did not defend himself at all until George had shouted at him repeatedly to fight back).

Slim exonerates Lennie, who is, once again, whimpering. Later, when Candy finds Curley's wife dead, his first thought is whether his own dream (his escape) can survive this huge setback.

So too, here, George asks Slim if they will be able to keep their jobs. Slim threatens and bullies Curley into an agreed version of events- suggesting that he, like Candy, injured his hand in a machine; that his injury is an occupational hazard of working on the ranch.

It is, in fact, debatable whether Slim would have the power to save George's and Lennie's jobs, but Curley gives in readily enough; it seems that the bully can be bullied himself, by Slim.

The scene ends, poignantly, with Lennie struggling to understand that George is not displeased with him, because his own show of strength was both reasonable and provoked.

We, the readers, understand the difference between naked aggression and self-defence; Lennie does not.

Section Four

This section takes place the following evening, Saturday. It starts with our introduction to Crooks. Like Curley's wife, but unlike the other characters, Crooks has had various things said about him earlier in the narrative, many of them racist. We know that he is black and that, because of this, he is not normally allowed in the bunkhouse, but he was allowed in at Christmas – although that was so that he could be exploited and made to fight.

Crooks has his own quarters, in a little shed that leaned off the wall of the barn". Candy had told George that Crooks reads a lot and has books in his room. It turns out that among those books are a tattered dictionary and a copy of the California civil code for 1905, which implies that Crooks is exact and varied with his language in a way the others are not, and that he has had cause to learn about civil rights. His disability bends his body to the left; presumably his injury, like Candy's, is an occupational one suffered on this ranch.

Crooks is territorial. When Lennie comes, to take an innocent, friendly interest in him, Crooks points out that, just as he can't come into the bunkhouse, he doesn't want anyone in is his room. He has to explain to Lennie the nature of his segregation, which is derogatory; he is not allowed to play cards in the bunkhouse. He gives the reason that the others say that he smells. This puts him on the same level as Candy's dog, because that was the complaint levelled against it too. The white ranch workers do not complain about each other's smells.

Lennie breaks down Crooks' objections and resentment, and they start to talk. Lennie discloses the dream to Crooks, who is acute enough to understand that much of what is said to Lennie is incomprehensible to him. Crooks' own father had a chicken ranch about the same size as the dream farm, and it was in California. But Crooks' own father had discouraged him from playing with white children, knowing they would start to discriminate against him before long.

He is isolated acutely by the scarcity of coloured people, and he is not heard or listened to. His loneliness is by virtue of his colour; Curley' wife's is by virtue of her gender. They should be natural allies, but she is even more vicious to Crooks than the men are.

Crooks torments Lennie with a cruel game, based on supposing that George does not come back for Lennie after his night in the town. His motivation is his own loneliness and isolation; he wants Lennie to feel what it is like to be utterly friendless. For Crooks, reading is in fact a reluctant pastime. It is not a substitute for companionship, but it is the best way he can manage his own isolation.

But Crooks, with the insight of the outcast, the underdog, also articulates a prophecy which could easily come to fruition; that Lennie, without George, would be treated as a lunatic.

This prefigures Slim's apprehension (which he uses to justify the mercy killing of Lennie) that the authorities would want to seize him, then lock him in a cage for others to mock. Crooks semi-soliloquises that loneliness can drive you mad; just as Lennie can't understand some of what people say, Crooks is no longer sure whether what he sees is true or real or not. His own dream is not of the future, but of the past, when he had two brothers on his own family's farm.

He is dismissive of Lennie's dream, because he has seen so many others with the same thought and ambition, but none of them ever made their dream come true. Frustration and loneliness always got the better of them, and they spent their money on gambling or women, instead of continuing to save enough to buy the land they need.

When Candy comes looking for Lennie, Crooks lets him into his room too. It is a poignant moment, because it breaks down a barrier which has always been taken for granted until now.

The two men are equally disabled, and perhaps equally abused. All that keeps them apart, and isolated in their loneliness, is the fact that one of them is white and the other black.

When Candy reveals to Crooks that they almost have the money they need, and are just a month away from buying the farm, his cynicism evaporates, and he offers to come and help, too. For George, the dream is about independence and relative comfort; for Lennie, about safety and rabbits; for Candy, about security in old age; and, for Crooks, about escaping from loneliness and segregation.

Once again, at a critical moment, where mutual co-operation may be on the point of making defensive individualism obsolete, Curley's wife appears in the doorway. This time, her usual conversation opener, (whether anyone has seen her husband) is pathetically ironic, because she knows that he too has gone into the town- which means a trip to the brothel. Candy and Crooks are hostile and avoid eye contact with her, but Lennie, predictably, is fascinated.

The scene is similar to her first appearance in Scene Two, but this time George is not there to protect Lennie. Her comment on how they left all the weak ones here is an expression of disappointment and hopelessness. Her body language shifts from coquettish to assertive, and she complains that when the men are in a pair or a group they will not talk to her.

Just as Crooks has explained why he is so lonely, and has taken his frustration out on Lennie with a cruel game, Curley's wife now does the same, to him. Perhaps because, after two weeks of marriage, her husband is in a brothel, she is scathing and sarcastic about Curley, who, she complains, only talks about how he is going to fell his enemies.

She is curious about Curley's damaged hand, and sceptical about the official story. Like Crooks, she digresses on to the subject of her own lost dream of being in the theatre or the film industry.

We might compare Curley's wife's verbal antagonising with Curley's physical aggression. Just as Slim and Carlson had stood up to him, Candy confronts her, saying that they may have been scared of getting sacked before, but no longer, because soon they will have their own place, which no one will be able to sack them from. She is derisive about the idea, and the men will say nothing more to her, but she sees that Lennie is embarrassed, and asks him about the damage to his face. She promises that she will talk to him later, and playfully suggests that she might get a rabbit or two of her own.

Crooks tries to bring the potentially dangerous exchange to a close, by telling her she has no right to be in his room or in the barn. Her response is vicious; she points out to him that she could get him strung up, if she so chose.

The context here is that if she were to accuse Crooks of a sexual assault, his colour would mean that he would never be given a fair hearing.

This is exactly the point which is dramatized so effectively in the court scene in Harper Lee's "To Kill a Mockingbird", where the wrongs of racism are many times more powerful than the rights of the law (Tom Robinson is convicted of a sexual assault purely out of racial prejudice).

She intimidates Candy, too; then, in a surprise close, she thanks Lennie for hurting Curley. It is something she'd thought about (because she hates him so!) but would never do. She knows that a man so quick to inflict violence should himself feel the force of it too.

George returns, and is dismayed both to find Lennie in Crooks' room and to discover that Candy has told Crooks about the farm. Candy says he has told no-one else- forgetting what he has just said to Curley's wife.

Crooks retracts his offer to help- his rough treatment at the hands of Curley's wife has reminded him of how unpleasant people with any degree of power tend to be towards black people- and the scene ends, symbolically, where it had started, with Crooks medicating his back.

Section Five

The action has moved on to Sunday afternoon. Lennie is in the barn while the other men are playing horseshoes. He has the puppy (he has accidentally killed it, by squeezing it too hard) with him, in the straw. He continues to stroke it; and he cannot understand how it, a creature bigger than a mouse, has died. Lennie fears that, if George finds out, he will not allow Lennie to tend the rabbits. He evaluates how bad a thing accidentally killing the puppy is, and decides it is not serious enough to warrant going to hide in the brush for safety.

Lennie has a premonition that George will know anyway- we have seen how George is always able to detect Lennie's attempts at concealing anything- and he experiences a George-like outburst of anger at the puppy for somehow being responsible for its own death (this foreshadows Candy's anger at Curley's wife after she has been killed).

He decides that the puppy wasn't big enough- which raises the question of how large a creature has to be, in order to survive Lennie's stroking. And, at this very moment, Curley's wife- a not particularly big or robust creature- comes very quietly into the barn. She is dressed exactly as she was when George and Lennie first saw her. This time, she makes no pretence of looking for Curley, but addresses Lennie in a familiar way, and points out to him that it is now pointless for George to ban him from talking to her for fear of Curley's power as a boxer, or as an employer, because that power has gone. Curley no longer has anything to back his threats up with.

She has sought Lennie out in order to have a conversation and counteract her loneliness. She overcomes his reluctance, by asking him about the puppy, and she angrily objects to the idea that she is not to be spoken to; she has no intention of harming him.

Lennie, of course, has no intention of harming her (but he does); and although she does not intend to harm him, her mere presence does. It is now that we begin to appreciate the full force of the idea behind the title of the novel; that intention counts for nothing, because death is often accidental.

Curley's wife has come to understand the fundamental problem of the limited and defensive way of life she has on the ranch, where no one cares about her or how she lives.

Now, in her frustration, her back story tumbles out. She relates her story own story to Lennie- her dream of being put in the movies, her mother's refusal to let her go at the age of fifteen, and the non-receipt of the audition letter from Hollywood, which she thinks her mother had stolen and withheld from her (there may have been no letter at all, of course).

Her decision to marry Curley was made in an instant, in a fit of pique, before she even knew him. She is vain and shallow and callow; but what she has found out is that Curley isn't nice either and that she does not even like him.

Lennie is still preoccupied with the problem of how to stay on the right side of George after killing the puppy, so that he can still have the rabbits; his head is full of long-hair rabbits; he moves closer to her, and she moves away a little. Then she makes what we know will be the fatal error; contrasting her own soft, fine hair with Curley's coarse and wiry hair, she invites Lennie to stroke it. He does at once and then, when he strokes harder, and when she demands that he stops, he panics.

When she screams, he tries to suppress the noise, because George will be mad – Lennie knows this, because this is what happened in Weed. The problem wasn't what Lennie was doing (he didn't do any more than touch a red dress) but how everything stepped up a gear once the girl screamed.

So, here, he will do whatever he has to, in order to prevent her screaming. He is angry, and does not recognise that, like a helpless small animal (such as the mouse of the title), her eyes are wild with terror. Just like

Curley's hand had done, she becomes floppy. Her neck is broken.

The tragic irony is that the very deterrent (anger, and a ban on tending rabbits) which was designed to prevent Lennie from getting into trouble is the cause of the killing which destroys so many dreams. Just like the quartet of puppies which Slim drowned, a quartet of dreams dies with Curley's wife- George's, Lennie's, her own, and Candy's.

The behaviour of Curley's wife is- predictably- exactly the same as that of another nameless girl, the one in Weed; and Lennie behaves exactly as we expect him to, and know he will. Curley's wife did not know about the Weed event, and she did not witness the crushing of Curley's hand. If she had, she would not have put herself in this situation. Her dream of film star celebrity, which had seemed to have no substance or evidence to support it, dies with her, unrealised, no nearer than it had ever been.

Lennie cannot differentiate between the dead puppy and the dead Curley's wife, on one level; he talks to both of them after they are dead, and covers both of them with hay. He realises that he must now hide in the brush till George comes, (because something serious has happened) but he thinks that if he takes the dead puppy with him, and disposes of it separately, things will be marginally less bad.

This unconventional set of values reminds us how different Lennie's perceptions are from everyone else's.

All the deaths in the novel are quick and apparently painless; we know that the symmetry will not be spoilt by Curley's threats a little further on, to shoot Lennie in the most painful way he can think of.

Looking for Lennie, because he too is obsessed now with the imminent plans for the farm, Candy finds Curley's wife, and he has no reason to think, at first, that she is dead. When he realises what has happened, Candy brings George back with him; George hopes that Lennie can be captured, because, left to his own devices, he will starve. Candy points out that Curley will want Lennie dead.

Where we would expect any normal human being to express shock and grief at the violent and avoidable death of a young woman, Candy is still obsessed with the farm, asking George to persevere with the farm purchase. George points out to him (out of honesty? or bitterness?) that the dream was never realistic; it only came to be believed in (like a statistic) through incessant repetition.

George plans to revert to the ordinary ranch-hand's life, and to do those things at the end of the month which his responsibility for Lennie has previously put beyond his reach. He realises the other men must know that Lennie is the killer, but he wants Candy to delay telling them, so that he can stage his own entrance and not be suspected of being involved.

This is so that George can be sure that he can take Carlson's pistol, and that he will be free to reach Lennie at the pool before Curley and the mob get there. He is absolutely determined that he will not let them hurt Lennie. At first, we may not be fully aware that the same fate (only differently executed) awaits Lennie. George could be motivated by the desire to protect Lennie, but not necessarily to kill him.

Left alone with the body, Candy addresses Curley's wife as both a tramp and a tart. He feels neither sorrow nor respect for her, but only resentment that, in her death, she has robbed him of the dream of security which buying the farm would have brought him. He is crying, but for himself, not at the tragedy of a very young woman meeting a sudden, violent death. He had called her a "tart" in Section Two; his opinion has not changed (though he was wrong); but now he resents her for the loss of the personal dream which he so nearly had the opportunity to realise.

When the other men arrive, Slim checks that she is indeed dead; and then Curley, without even a nano-second of grief or reflection, goes straight to the opportunity for revenge on Lennie (for his hand as much as his wife). In this culture, where violence is the only means of resolving conflict, and the idea is to hit the person who has hit you back twice as hard, he is determined to kill Lennie, and to have the satisfaction of doing it himself. Curley is never more at home than as the leader of a bloodthirsty gang which consists of Carlson and Whit; Candy, Crooks and George are in the background, and will try to deal with the crisis more sensibly.

Slim confirms with George that Lennie is the culprit, and he connects this latest episode with the event in Weed which George had related to him in all its detail. Slim sighs, and makes his judgment that Lennie must be killed. Slim knows that Curley will be determined to shoot Lennie, in revenge, not for his wife, but for his hand. And, even if they could restrain Curley, Lennie's future would consist of being strapped down and put in a cage, because there is no provision in this society for people who are unable to take full responsibility for their actions.

Slim is just as calm and poised here as he was when he had to decide that Candy's dog should be shot. It is a complex decision which properly belongs to a court, but the combination of the "Wild West" culture of violence and the lack of interest in, or provision for, people like Lennie simplifies it. Today, we would expect someone like Lennie to be allowed to plead guilty to manslaughter on the grounds of diminished responsibility; the next steps would be dictated by the need to protect the public, not the lust for revenge. Lennie would be held in a secure hospital, not put in a cage or a freak show.

When we read this almost casual death sentence, we are not surprised, in the sense that we recognise that the shooting of Candy's dog was its precursor. But we also feel morally offended; the punishment does not fit the "crime". The perfect storm of events has meant that George's conscientious efforts to keep Lennie out of trouble have failed; the best laid plans of mice and men have indeed gone awry.

This is the point where the novel becomes tragic, although it is not, in strict terms, a tragedy in the Aristotelian sense, or in the sense we use to define the term. In "tragedy", the hero loses his place in society because of a fatal flaw in his character which is expressed in arrogant or hubristic behaviour.

In Shakespeare, Macbeth's murder of all who could stop his descendants' path to the throne means that society can no longer tolerate him. King Lear should have been wise before he was old; in misjudging his daughters, and testing their professions of love for him in a competitive game, he finds out what he should have taken more care of, goes mad, and dies of grief.

Lennie does not have a conscious intention to harm Curley's wife, the puppy or the various mice. He simply does not understand his own physical, brute strength, and his imperfect memory makes it impossible for him to learn from past experiences and mistakes. In fact, he abhors aggression.

<u>The tragedy of the novel is not, in the final analysis, Lennie's; it is the tragedy of the society he lives in, which cannot find a way of providing for or accommodating people like him. Tragic heroes so offend the society</u>

they live in that they lose their place in it. So does Lennie; but he has no tragic flaw in his character.

Carlson is excited that his Luger gun has gone missing (George has taken it, as a means of protecting Lennie from suffering at the hands of Curley and his mob). He assumes that Lennie has taken it, in order to defend himself against his pursuers. We know that Lennie is not interested in stealing anything from anybody, but it may be right to say that in the heat of the moment here- the narrative is moving very quickly- we do not realise straight away that it is George who has it, or why; George's intentions are not necessarily clear to us, especially on a first reading.

There is scope for the reader to experience the same momentary confusion here as some of the characters.

Curley's anger, we are told, has grown colder. In case there is a Wild West shootout he tells the others to arm themselves, using, for example, Crooks' shotgun. He despatches Whit to fetch the deputy sheriff, and he regards George with suspicion. George tries to plead with Curley not to shoot Lennie, but, because Curley assumes that Lennie has Carlson's gun, he is as remorseless as Carlson had been over the need (or opportunity) to shoot Candy's dog; and he seeks vengeance for the crushing of his hand.

Slim suggests that Curley stays with his wife (which would leave Carlson as Lennie's only real pursuer) but Curley is bent on revenge, cannot be deflected, and sees it as a personal issue; Slim drops the challenge, and George has, reluctantly, to go with Curley, who insists on it, to prove that he was not Lennie's accessory to murder. Curley wants George to witness his gruesome revenge on Lennie.

The last line of this scene sees Candy lying in the hay with his arm covering his eyes. This is the same inertia in the face of something violent and out of his control that he had exhibited while he waited for Carlson to shoot his dog; now he is waiting, weakly, for Lennie to be shot, like his dog.

Section Six

The final scene of the novel uses calculated repetition of the description of the pool to take us back to the opening scene. There is a sense of things coming full circle; this is where the story began and this is where it will end. We remember that George and Lennie arrived here with their dream, and we know that the dream, which had come agonisingly close to being achieved, is as dead as Lennie's puppy and Curley's wife.

We come to this scene with forebodings about what will happen here. It is another day in the world of nature. In the second paragraph, the heron kills the helpless, unsuspecting water snake casually and with force. We are onlookers; it is presented to us in a matter-of-fact way, and there is nothing we can do to prevent it.

The wind drives through the tops of the trees, and then dies. There is a two-fold analogy here. George and Lennie were here less than three days ago, with their relationship as well as their dream, and this is the place where their friendship is about to die. Lennie had come crashing through the undergrowth here, before they slept under the stars; the lynch party will crash through the brush, and then the wind of Lennie's life and breath will die.

There is a symbolic dimension to this too. The wind blows, but the landscape settles back to how it has always been. Nature itself is indifferent to the cycle of life and cruel, sudden death. We know that the world of the pool and the ranch will only be disturbed for a moment or two by the violent events which involve Lennie. Afterwards, everything will be the same as before. Nothing will have been learnt.

In the fourth paragraph, the heron stands motionless as a second water snake approaches, in exactly the same way as the one which it has just swallowed. Why should this second water snake escape the same fate? Perhaps Steinbeck intends us to think of the heron as death; it has taken Curley's wife, and now it will take Lennie.

Lennie appears, moving like a creeping bear, He is silent, partly to avoid being detected, and bear-like because his strength and the lumbering slowness is what defines him to us. Even so, the noise he makes is enough to distract the heron, which flies off, sparing the second water snake, for now. We wonder for a brief moment whether perhaps there is a chance that Lennie may also escape with his life.

He drinks from the pool, but where, in the first scene, he submerged his head and hat, in pure, innocent joy, now his lips barely touch the water; he is nervous, uncomfortable, wary. His sitting position apes the position George took after he had drunk from the pool in Scene One, a position Lennie copied carefully; only, this time, George is not here to protect him.

Lennie's response to George's displeasure over the dead mouse and the history of trouble had been to offer to go off by himself and live in the mountains. George had dismissed the idea as impractical; Lennie has no survival skills. Now the same thought occupies Lennie; he is pleased with himself for remembering George's instruction to come back here and wait for him, but he worries that George will finally have given up on him.

Now, Steinbeck builds the dramatic tension with another of his sudden and unexpected diversions; the extraordinary appearance of Aunt Clara, who appears as a vision to Lennie, speaks in Lennie's own voice, and expresses the guilt he feels over the burden he is to George. Then, out of Lennie's head again, there comes a gigantic rabbit, which also speaks like Lennie, but, like the Aunt Clara figure, uses the language George uses. The rabbit taunts Lennie, as Crooks had done, with the threat that George will abandon him, or with the threat of Curley-like violence.

Taken together, these two cartoon-like characters externalise Lennie's disturbed thoughts and his inability to make sense of everything that has happened. We understand how he suffers because he cannot please George for long, or live a trouble-free life.

As Lennie calls out for George in distress, George arrives and speaks to him quietly.

Lennie takes up the rabbit's threat, that George will leave him, and asks George whether it is true. This is the language less of friends than of a long-term intimate romantic relationship. George tends here to be silent, because he cannot offer Lennie reassurance (it would be dishonest to do so), and because he is weighed down by the magnitude of what he knows he will have to do.

Lennie (like the little water snake) has no sense of the danger he is in; he wants George to recite the familiar routine about how he could have an easier life without him, now that George has confirmed that he will not abandon him. George hears the lynch party in the distance, and tries to judge how near it is; Lennie is oblivious to it, and to the wooden and monotonous, uninflected tone in which George is speaking to him.

George's words to Lennie- "I want you to stay with me"- are exactly the same as the phrase he used three times here on Thursday evening, but the reason why George wants him to stay- so that he can kill him mercifully and painlessly- is completely different.

Lennie presses George to recite the dream, because that is the sequence of the conversation that they had had before, when Lennie offered to go off to live in the hills and George became ashamed of his own meanness. Again, Lennie is exultant about the sense of belonging with another person- he cries happily, and these are cries in the sense of shouts, not tears.

As Curley and the search party approaches, the dramatic tension increases- we know, as George knows, that Lennie's time is running out. But our emotional involvement here comes less from the dramatic tension- we know the eventual outcome in advance- than from the dramatic irony.

Lennie still thinks that the comfort he finds in the familiar verbal routines means that life will continue as before. He thinks that the clearing is a place of safety, and that George has come to rescue him as he did in Weed. He simply has no real awareness of the consequences of killing Curley's wife-perhaps because the accidental killing of smaller animals has never done more than disrupt the pattern of George's protection and approval for a short time.

George takes his hat off, and tells Lennie to do the same; he knows that Lennie will copy his movements. As Curley can be heard getting nearer, Lennie is still focused on the dream; he seems, already, to have forgotten the death of Curley's wife completely.

Each phrase Lennie says to George now – especially when he asks him to tell him how lovely 'it' is now going to be - is laden with irony, because it means something very different to us and to George from what it means to Lennie. The "it" Lennie asks about is having the farm, but to George and us it is the shooting of Lennie.

It takes George two attempts to carry it out, even under the pressure of knowing that Curley is about to arrive. Just as Carlson killed Candy's dog, kindly, leading the obedient animal outside gently to a fate it did not anticipate, George stresses to Lennie that he is not angry with him.

The shooting itself is described accurately, but with the minimum of graphic detail. There is no mention of blood, for example, or if Lennie cried out.

In describing the now dead Lennie, the narrative says only that he isn't quivering. Steinbeck does this because the focus is on why Lennie was killed; there is no room or time in the plot to go into how (presumably) George may have been affected by the grim physicality of shooting someone, and how he may or may not have changed his mind about whether what he did was indeed a better or worse thing than the alternative. As I noted at the beginning of this guide, Steinbeck's characters can speak; but they cannot really do much thinking, as a general rule.

So Steinbeck keeps us on practicalities here. Curley is interested only in confirming to himself that Lennie is dead.

George has to exonerate himself by pretending to Carlson that Lennie had his gun, and that he shot him in self-defence. This allows Carlson and Curley to keep, undisturbed, their view of Lennie as that "big bastard", not as the kind, loyal, simple and only accidentally harmful creature he really was. No-one other than George could possibly appreciate Lennie's essential gentleness and lack of aggression; and no-one is interested in re-evaluating, or reaching a better understanding of, other people.

Slim simply keeps confirming to George that he has done the right thing. He alone knows what has happened, and he alone understands George's anguish.

George and Slim are the only two characters in the novel who have any compassion and any interest in why others behave as they do. In their capacity to understand emotion, they are less animalistic and more humane than Curley and the others; but they are still living in that world.

There is a possibility that a true friendship might develop between them (Slim had spoken approvingly of the friendships that the ranch workers never have, because of their isolation and mistrust).

The novel ends with Carlson demonstrating that no-one else has the capacity to understand, or to see the need to do things differently. Simple violence suffices; two wrongs make a right.

Carlson, as a symbol of the ranch-hands' way of life, is condemned out of his own mouth.

Themes and analysis

Now that we have covered the plot and expanded on why the writer chooses words as he does, we are ready to unpick themes.

For both OCR and AQA candidates this is most important. There is a high likelihood that you main exam question will suggest a particular, unifying theme, then ask you to comment on how it is illustrated in the narrative.

A theme, in many ways, is simply a line of thought which is repeated or developed throughout the telling of a story (like the chorus of a song).

So it will help you to be prepared for possible questions, if you have thought about the issues that recur at various points throughout the text, and if you can trace how they gather emotional power.

Remember, the examiner is interested in what you think and feel – this isn't maths with a right or wrong answer. What counts is supporting your point of view with evidence from the text, so that the examiner can see your logic.

Let's start with the most 'obvious' question first – what the writer is actually trying to say, overall.

What is "Of Mice and Men" really about?

Your first reaction to this question might be to say that the answer is obvious; the novel is about George and Lennie and what happens to these two characters, and so on.

But there is a big difference between what is in the book and what the book is really about.

Lennie accidentally kills Curley's wife, and, as a consequence of that, George shoots Lennie, to save him from a worse death at the hands of Curley. Is it right that Lennie dies in this way? Is it right that Lennie dies at all?

Steinbeck creates, in Lennie, a man who cannot understand the threat he poses to other people, because he does not appreciate his own strength. Moreover, he cannot learn from past mistakes, because his memory is imperfect. He can remember simple instructions for a short length of time, but little more than that. We see him reciting commands over and over to himself, so that he can internalise George's instructions.

Lennie is in George's hands, and, without a welfare or benefits system to support either of them, George has to work in a low-paid agricultural job, and so does Lennie. It is not possible to keep Lennie away from other people; nor is it possible to keep him among people who know him, because the work is short-term and they have to move from one location to another.

Lennie is, as we might put it today, an accident waiting to happen (or, more accurately, after the episode in Weed, an accident which has already happened more than once).

Could Lennie have avoided killing Curley's wife? It is clear that we cannot judge him by the standards we would use with other people, because he does not have the necessary human capacity to learn from past mistakes; his appreciation of danger is limited. He has no intention of harming her, and his fascination with soft things leads him into a situation where he cannot control the outcome.

If Lennie is not to blame for the death of Curley's wife, is someone else responsible for it?

Take, as a start, a theory some people put forward as their first response to this question- the idea that perhaps Curley's wife was, in fact, responsible for her own death. She would not have died if she had not been there, after all. But we can dismiss this, because she would never have allowed herself to be alone with Lennie if she had known his history of petting soft things to death; but she knows nothing of that aspect of his behaviour, and nor can we expect her to.

She speaks to him because she is desperately lonely. She is lonely because the men on the ranch are afraid of her and will not talk to her, partly because she is married to Curley, the boss's son, and partly because, as a woman, she is a dangerous temptation to the men ("jail bait").

She married Curley, not knowing that he was a thug, interested only in fighting, and with no skills in relationships and no real interest in her except as a possession (hence the fact that she has no name of her own). She married him in order to escape from her own childhood home, where she felt her mother was actively preventing her from achieving her own dream.

This is not the first teenage rebellion in history, and it won't be the last. She is the victim of her own naiveté and immaturity, but those are not criminal qualities; she is also the victim of Lennie's physical strength. We cannot blame her for what she did not and could not know.

If George had been with Lennie, he would not have been alone with Curley's wife in the barn. But George has made huge compromises in his own life, because of the obligation he feels to look after Lennie; he is constantly trying to keep Lennie out of trouble. It would be very harsh to hold him responsible for what Lennie does on the very rare occasions when he is doing something else.

110

Is it Curley's fault, then, that Lennie is killed? It is because Curley is so determined to kill Lennie, in as terrifying way as he can, that George has to step in and shoot Lennie first. Curley has had his hand crushed by Lennie, after he had picked on Lennie in a cowardly way; he relishes the prospect of revenge, and Lennie has killed his wife. If Lennie is impaired by his poor memory and understanding, Curley is impaired, too, by his one-dimensional aggressiveness.

Although he sends for the deputy sheriff, he intends to take the law into his own hands. This is wrong, but it is true to his own personality and temperament; he knows no other way to behave. The world of the ranch is one where the values are "an eye for an eye, a tooth for a tooth", and where arguments are settled by violence; and there is no sign that other boss's sons on other ranches have different values.

It is Slim who decides that Lennie must die, because any attempt to keep him alive would consign him to a life in captivity, in an asylum or a cage, which would be worse than death. Slim had also determined that

Candy's dog should be shot, because Carlson's objections to keeping it alive were stronger than Candy's loyalty. Although that was a hard decision, it is not presented as a bad one; in the world of the ranch, it is a practical solution to a difficult choice. Slim would not allow Lennie to be shot if he could protect him from Curley, or if he could be found a tolerable place in the community. Once those options prove impossible, there really is only one option left.

George delivers the fatal shot, but he kills Lennie for humane reasons, not impulsively or angrily. We see how deeply affected by this George is; Lennie was difficult to protect, and ultimately George has failed to protect him, but Lennie brought a sense of purpose and validity to George's life which will be missing without him. George has no desire or motive to kill Lennie, other than to save him from a painful execution at the hands of the uncontrollable Curley.

Shooting Lennie is humane; it is also self-sacrificing, because it consigns George to the lower way of life he had felt he had, with his relationship with Lennie, risen above.

No-one would argue that Candy or Crooks is responsible for Lennie's death; he was friends with both of them. He had no argument with Carlson.

We are left with only one conclusion; that no individual is to blame for Lennie's death. Steinbeck goes to great trouble to construct a plot in which what happens is unavoidable, though accidental. We know what the characters do not (the whole story); if we are powerless to prevent Lennie's death, so are they.

Lennie's death is, therefore, the result and the fault of the society he lives in- a society devoid of a sense of compassion, or community, or any insight into the needs of the vulnerable, or how to look after them.

We know from the outset that, just as everything had gone wrong in Weed, George and Lennie are driven, by their need for money (to buy a small farm, improve their own lives and gain the peace and independence which would guarantee Lennie's safety in the future), into another location where Curley and Curley's wife are both threats of trouble and disaster.

We know, from the title of the novel, and from the way Steinbeck develops the narrative, with the shooting of Candy's dog, that this tale will not- cannot- end well.

Shooting Candy's dog is the act of the primitive society; when something takes some looking after, you get rid of it. The same principle evidently applies to people as well as animals; Candy is similar to his dog, and the same fate, of being a cast-off, cut adrift when he no longer serves any useful purpose, awaits him in the near future.

While Candy concedes that he will not actually be shot, the bleak picture he presents of what awaits people like him who can no longer earn a wage carries the implication of a short and unhappy life in so-called retirement. There is no life after work for these workers.

Nobody on the ranch has a store of happy memories to draw on. There seems to be only the present, which is insecure or unhappy, and the future, which is worse, or no better than the present. Perhaps this explains the need for dreams, for all of those hundreds of men whom Crooks and Curley's wife have seen passing through.

The dream is the escape clause. But these dreams, as those characters' failures demonstrate, and as the narrative of the novel proves, do not- ever- come true.

In his state of constant readiness to launch a pre-emptive attack on anyone he feels threatened by, Curley is also primitive; a caveman. In spite of the occasional passing reference to the deputy sheriff and to San Quentin prison, the prevailing sense in the novel is of lawlessness.

Candy's copy of the California civil code is dated 1905, so it is well out of date, indeed by more than 25 years. We have the sense that any legal framework is distant and inaccessible to people on the ranches; men have to sort their problems out for and among themselves. The mob in Weed, and Curley's methods of exacting justice, speak to us of a still brutal and Wild West. If Lennie were to run to the mountains, he would not survive; but Steinbeck wants the threat of a final, dramatic shoot-out (though it is not a set-piece battle) in order to bring out the theme of rough justice in a rough and primitive world. The fact that it becomes an unopposed execution ironically denies the men involved- the readers of Western magazines- the blazing climax they would expect and enjoy.

The novel was published in 1937. It does not have a precise historical timing, but Murray and Ready are operating under Roosevelt's "New Deal", which sets it in the early 1930s. Thus, Steinbeck is saying to the reader that this is what is happening or could be happening, even now, in modern America; that, amid the mechanisation of farming, and the genesis of the film industry, this kind of primitivism still goes on.

It is both in the world of Nature, which he shows us as red in tooth and claw, and unnatural. The peace of the clearing is shattered by the gunshot which kills Lennie, but here the deaths of dogs, of water snakes, of young women- of anyone- are barely remarked upon, as the hard business of staying alive demands all of everyone's daily care and effort. Human life and mouse life are as precarious and fragile as each other.

Steinbeck is asking us "What sort of world is it that operates like this; where Lennie has to die?" He is asking us what we can do, or will do, to make sure that such injustices cannot occur in the world we live in- in our country, our region, our town. He is asking us how fine the line is between the supposed civilisation of a modern society and the raw savagery of the natural world.

This question of how far we have really evolved, or how far we are from a world of nature, where there is no pretence of a caring society, is a recurring theme in great literature. It is at the heart of Shakespeare's tragedy "King Lear". Because violence and victimisation breaks out, from time to time, in all societies, at all times, in all parts of the world, it remains relevant to us today and is still widely read, long after the world of the agricultural labourer in 1930s California has gone.

Steinbeck treated some of the themes in "Of Mice and Men" at greater length in his epic novel "The Grapes of Wrath", which appeared only two years later, in 1939. In that work, he explores the economic powerlessness of the unskilled manual worker, and warns that too much poverty and deprivation will eventually force decent people who have no hope of supporting themselves by peaceful means to take land and wealth by force.

The American Dream – and what Steinbeck thinks about it

America was a young country, and in the early years of the 20th century it attracted migrants from all over Europe, on the basis that anyone, regardless of their background or wealth, could go there and make their way in a democratic, meritocratic land of opportunity.

The hardship of the Great Depression tested the validity of this notion, and it has pre-occupied many American writers ever since. F Scott Fitzgerald's famous novel "The Great Gatsby", published in 1926, deals with a variation on this theme; Jay Gatsby is a rich, but not quite respectable, man whose "new money" leaves him an outsider, and, eventually, a fatal casualty of the "old money" world he joins in order to try to rekindle an old romance with the one love of his life.

Even before the Great Depression, American society had become rigid, according to Fitzgerald's portrayal; where there is capital, or wealth, those who have it are determined to hold on to it, and many of them become cruel and selfish. There is a glass ceiling, and the notion of opportunity for all bears no relation to the reality.

A dream, in the sense of a driving motivation to achieve a particular, specific aim, is a very powerful ingredient or resource for a novelist, because novels will often involve a difficult journey of development for the hero of the story, and their dream gives them the strength to overcome the apparently impossible obstacles the novel puts in their way.

In the two novels I have mentioned, just as in "Of Mice and Men", the dream proves impossible to achieve, and pursuing it leads to personal tragedy for those involved- the Joad family, Gatsby, George and Lennie. In each case, the protagonist or hero pursues their dream to the point of their own destruction, long after their own experience should have taught them to abandon it. But dreams are obsessive, and not easily given up.

Do good novels go out of date?

We're used to the idea that food has "use by" dates and "best before" dates. Does the passing of time make novels any less safe to "eat", or any less easy to "digest"?

Charity shops are full of novels which have not lived beyond their own time. The more they fit the flavour of the month, and the less they have to say, the shorter books' shelf lives will be.

On the other hand, we still read Chaucer, Shakespeare, Jane Austen, Dickens, George Orwell; we still listen to Bach, Mozart and Beethoven. This isn't mere convention. Something about the content still speaks to us over spans of time much longer than the 75 years or so since Steinbeck wrote "Of Mice and Men".

Many people feel that some aspects of Steinbeck's message no longer resonate with us quite as he intended; this is not, however, his fault.

We live in a more industrial age. We have sophisticated welfare and benefits systems, and higher standards of living than Steinbeck's labourers. Global travel means that we can go further afield to escape poverty and build our own future. The class system seems less entrenched, because, in our western world at least, there is less absolute poverty (just read the second half of "The Grapes of Wrath" and you'll see what I mean).We have seen the benefits of organised labour and big company culture; we have seen their faults, too, and, as I write this in 2014, the trend seems to be towards small business, flexible working, working from home.

Those who believe that the world owes any of us a living are losing the battle; and acquiring new skills, as demand changes, is probably easier now than ever before.

So we do not face the dilemma of Steinbeck's working men; find the same sort of work you've always done, in a shrinking market, or starve. We understand the drawbacks and the corruptibility of capitalism, but we have also seen the failure of the communist polar opposite. Social mobility means that we feel less resentful than previous generations of those who may have more than us.

Globalisation may catch the developed world out, in the same way that mechanisation lowered the economic value of farm labour in California in the 1930s; but we have more resources, more nimbleness to find a way of dealing with that.

If not yet, then fairly soon, readers of Steinbeck will start to find his characterisation rather idealised and too romantic. The description of Slim is the clearest example. Here is a man whose skill with a bull-whip elevates him to a god-like position among the unskilled. In a world where skills are very diverse, and well distributed, such a distinction begins to feel artificial and simplistic.

Would a Curley be so intimidating in our world? As an employer, he would not have the same degree of power over a more mobile and les dependent workforce. Would Curley's wife be so trapped? We are used to people reinventing themselves, walking away from bad relationships, and striking out on their own.

Most of all, we are becoming unused to the idea that our economy and our prosperity is built on the labour of an exploited working class. Mining disasters take place nowadays in Chile and Turkey, but not in the UK, because we no longer mine on an industrial scale.

Education after the age of 16 has relieved us of the stark lack of hope Steinbeck depicts as the norm. We have a minimum wage, and we have tax credits; we have care homes, and supermarkets which now employ the over-65s. We have safety nets which protect us from many of the risks which impoverish Steinbeck's people, not only financially but emotionally.

That's not to say that slave labour is extinct, in either the developed or the developing world. But there is measurable protection from exploitation to a degree that Steinbeck's characters would have wondered at.

Just as the glamourising of the "working class"- a sector we are absorbing into a broader definition of class- has been in and out of fashion over the past half-century, but is less of a live concern now for many of us, Steinbeck's notion of the moral purpose of the writer is beginning to seem narrow and didactic nowadays. His detractors have always accused him of a cartoonish instinct towards the one-dimensional; a simplistic approach which overvictimises the victims and overdemonises the demons.

While "Of Mice and Men" bears the stamp of authenticity, in terms of the dialect, thinking and behaviour of its characters, there is an undercurrent of preachiness and a one-dimensionality in the narrative style which, as time goes on, will be regarded first as unconvincing, then as lacking in subtlety and elegance, and then lacking in realism- because today's readers' experience has moved such a long way from the experience of readers in the 1930s.

Critics will start to question, for example, whether characters can really survive and maintain their morale when they deny themselves any friendships. As the power of racism recedes, the inability, for years, of Crooks and Candy to converse with each other will start to seem like a historical anachronism, rather than a realistic possibility.

Each succeeding generation of readers will have to make slightly more allowance for the historic differences between the society Steinbeck presents and their own. And, unless we cultivate, in the next generations of readers, the ability to discern and reinterpret Steinbeck's central concerns- the abuse of the powerless, the blinding insecurity we feel, and the temptation not to care- he will become a historical, rather than a contemporary author.

As the distance between the time of the novel and our own time lengthens, then the question of representation starts to enter the critical process. We have to address a new dimension; what was Steinbeck saying in his time, and what is the equivalent issue today (because it will not be the same)? In many senses, this is welcome; it asks us to be more (re-)creative, and it should lead to

a new generation of critical approaches-
and study guides.

While we are not yet quite at that stage, I
want to leave teachers and students alike
with this challenge. It's easy to recognise
when we feel on the same side as
Steinbeck; but when we find him tiresome,
or simplistic, do we understand to what
extent that's because he is those things; or
to what extent do we feel that because his
world is not the world we ourselves know
and live in?

"Of Mice and Men" on film – what does this offer to the GCSE student?

There are two feature film versions of Steinbeck's novel. The first was made in 1939 by Hal Roach Studios, and was nominated for four Academy Awards. There are some striking differences from the book. Curley's wife is given a name (Mae) and she is leaving him after Lennie crushes his hand. All of the racist issues are censored- the film leaves out her intimidation of Crooks, for example. The end of the film makes no attempt to realise Lennie's vision of Aunt Clara and the giant rabbit. There is a sheriff on the hunt for Lennie, and George hands him Carlson's gun; there seems to be some sort of law and order framing the action.

The film concentrates on the loneliness of Curley's wife, and enlarges the role of the boss. It adds a wordless scene in which he and Curley slurp their food and ignore her. She is frustrated but immature.

The film glosses over the social issues which are so central to Steinbeck. The vulnerability of Lennie and the insecurity of working as an agricultural labourer are missing. There is no sense of irony or of the narrative's compassion for the characters. It is not a film which prompts any thoughts of social change. Instead, it takes Steinbeck's plot and presents it as a straightforward tale of the Wild West.

Gary Sinise's 1992 version does not pretend to be a literal version. Its strength is the performance of John Malkovich as Lennie, whose cognitive difficulties are touchingly clear. Again, the racism of Curley's wife is left out completely, in the interests of making her empathetic throughout. George shoots Lennie without any immediate pressure from the pursuing mob. Slim does not have the presence Steinbeck gives him. Life on the ranch is not as hard or hopeless as it is in the novel.

As with the 1939 version, there is no attempt to realise Lennie's visions in the final scene, and the sense of suspense is truncated; we miss any sense that Lennie's death is outrageous. The dream does not have the resonance Steinbeck gives it, and Candy shows no bitterness at losing it. The characters in general seem much less oppressed; there always seems to be another job to go to, and the sense of living a fragile, desperate existence has been filtered out.

No film (in this case, both versions run to 106 minutes) will ever be able to condense a novel without leaving a great deal out. The question for the student of the novel is how faithful the film version is to the spirit of the novel; the differences will be a significant clue to the essence of the narrative, but not to the essence of the writer's meaning or message.

The experience of this novel on film shows that as a story it can stand up without the element of social commentary. Even the 1939 version does not attempt to disturb us over the morality of the world the action is set in. The dignity and the pathos of characters such as Crooks and Candy is weaker. The economic insecurity attracts little interest from the directors, and the racism none at all.

Most significantly, Lennie's shooting is presented as affecting George-sentimentally- but it is not tragic in any sense; we do not feel that the other characters should feel the need to reflect on it, or that it has a deeper meaning. There is none of the slowing of the pace in the final scene, or the building of dramatic tension, which is so resonant in the novel.

To some extent, this is to do with the difficulty of transferring a novel into a different medium, such as film. But why is neither director interested in the racism issue, or in giving the loss of several characters' dreams more power? There is no hint, either, that the mechanisation of farming is about to end this way of living and working, or what the consequences of that might be.

There is scope for film directors to slow the action down, for dramatic effect, and to intensify the viewer's discomfort. In practice, these films do not lead us to an understanding that the characters are symbolic or representative of anything larger than themselves.

Acting styles change, too; the difference in the depth of the characterisation of Lennie is interesting, but each portrayal is very much in line with the expectations of the time when the film is made. Curley's wife is more sympathetic all the way through both films than Steinbeck makes her; some of the feeling we should have for Lennie is diverted in her direction. Both directors dispense with the literary weight of the nature settings, the technique of foreshadowing, and the possibility of a friendship between Slim and George, based on their shared understanding of social leadership and of responsibility to others.

Once we understand that the literary methods, which are so important to our understanding of the novel, are the last thing film directors are interested in, the film versions become useful to us, not because of the way they present the tale, but because of the way they highlight the differences between Steinbeck's voice and his interests and the priorities of films, which have to tell the story in so much less time and depth.

The films are an interesting supplement to reading Steinbeck's text, but there are some very significant differences; you should not rely on either of the film versions as a substitute for the written novel, because so much of Steinbeck's own voice is missing from both of them.

Your GCSE exam- what you need to know

If you are studying "Of Mice and Men" for AQA or OCR, you will have to answer one question, and you will have 45 minutes to plan, write and check your response. The question is in two parts - there is a passage to analyse and comment on, and then a more broadly based question, to test your understanding of the text as a whole.

The WJEC sets a paper which allows 60 minutes for the same type of task.

Each exam board has a website where you can see the questions set in previous years, become familiar with, and understand, how answers are marked, and read the examiners' reports.

Those reports highlight the strengths and weaknesses of each year's scripts. From them, we can make a list of positive and negative points; more of that in a moment.

The AQA exam will print a passage and ask you to use it to explain and analyse *how* a character (Curley or Crooks or Slim or

Curley's wife, for example) or a group of characters (women, farm labourers) is presented; or *how* some aspect of life is shown to us (friendship, loneliness, hardship, exploitation, dreams).

A question of this type is designed to see whether you can select the important details from a short passage and show how they help to construct the larger meaning in the novel. The emphasis is *on what we are shown.* This tests our understanding of Steinbeck's broader values and the moral issues (crime and punishment, social responsibility, fairness, discrimination, the use and abuse of power) he wants us to think about.

Try to develop a clear understanding of the role of each character, by asking yourself what would be missing from the novel if that character were not there?

If you do this, you will be ready to answer questions on the way Steinbeck represents issues, through his treatment of themes and through his characters.

OCR questions have tended to be rather different. They often ask us to explain and analyse *how and why we respond* emotionally to a particular episode; in other words, how conscious we are of what Steinbeck does with language. The issue "how does he do this" asks us to explain what lies behind the lines, not just what the passage says.

Sensible analysis of foreshadowing and symbolism will help you here. Look, too, for the words and phrases which have the most resonance, and lead us to be involved with the action emotionally (we sympathise with the weak).

The key skills here are showing that we can analyse Steinbeck's purpose, and that we can explain how and why we, as readers, respond as we do. What is he putting into our minds, and why?

In the OCR exam, you will have a choice; a passage-based question, which will be about Steinbeck's language and methods, or a novel-wide question which asks you to show how well you understand the themes of the narrative as a whole.

This is often best analysed by commenting on the choice of particular words or phrases, and tone of voice- how characters speak, at a particular point, as well as what they say. George, for example, may speak to Lennie fondly, or frustratedly; we always need to be clear about the characters' feelings, and about our feelings about theirs. Commenting on adverbs is often a good place to start with the language of the novel.

Examiners' reports stress that marks are given for commenting on what is in the passage- so we have to have *evidence* for our view. This means that there is a rule you should follow- if it isn't in the novel, leave it out!! Good evidence will be backed up with quotations. It is often enough to quote a short phrase, or even a single word, to prove your point.

The best answers will also avoid over-interpreting detail, but will start by observing details, will have sound and interesting things to say about why Steinbeck has chosen them, and may draw from that some wider conclusions about the context in which he was writing.

Markers are always interested in your personal response (provided it's sensible, and explained) so, for example, don't be afraid to analyse where and why you feel uncomfortable with what a character says or how they say it. The way Carlson treats Candy's dog and the way Curley's wife threatens Crooks are good examples of this.

More broadly, it is important to avoid repetition, because it suggests you have too little to say. What is important is your focus on the question. Identify key words in the question, and don't answer some other question you would have preferred to find! If you are answering a question about a set passage, write about that passage- refer to other episodes for evidence to prove your points, but keep your focus firmly on the passage in front of you.

You will be much less likely to lose marks for irrelevant material if you PLAN your answer carefully and thoroughly before you write it.

There is always a strong temptation to start writing straight away, in a timed exam- especially if you see people around you doing just that. But the exam allows time to plan, and it is almost impossible to get a really good mark without a really good plan.

If you have read the book, and taken a little time to think about what it means to say to us, you will have plenty of good material.

The test in the exam is, then, to choose the right material, put it into an effective structure, and use your points to construct an argument, which you support by reference to the text.

Let's take an example. Suppose the question says "Explain the significance of the shooting of Candy's dog".

First, bullet-point your ideas.

-Candy's dog has no usefulness, so it is a burden/problem

-violence and a lack of compassion apply

-Candy's affection for his dog is overruled

-the mob rules

-there is a clumsy attempt to comfort Candy, but the men are bad at expressing emotion

-Lennie will be treated in much the same way

-differences are resolved in a primitive way

-people are treated like animals

Seven or eight points are likely to be enough, because you will then need to develop them, and show why they are important.

For example, take the third point in our list-

The men on the ranch do not become close friends, because the labourers are casual workers who have no job security and move from one farm to another (like the blacksmith Whitey, whose bed George takes over). Candy is lower in status even than them; his injury prevents him from working in the fields, so he has only his dog for company. Because their relationships are so simple and unemotional, Carlson, the others and even Slim do not appreciate what Candy's dog means to him. They have no concept of a caring relationship with another person, let alone a pet.

You should develop each of your points in one paragraph. Try to use fairly short sentences. When you have finished, go on to your next point. Then write a summary/concluding paragraph to say which point is most important, and why.

Before you start writing your answer, put your points in order of importance, and write about them in order, with the most important first. Keep going. If you run out of time for that question, you must move on to the next one; it matters less to have left out your least important point than your most important one.

Don't try to write too much, but constantly check that *what you are writing is relevant to the question.*

And before you take the exam, ask your teacher to explain again how the mark scheme works. Then you will have at the front of your mind your understanding of what you will be given marks for, and what you won't.

Especially if you are to take your GCSE in summer 2015, I wish you every success.

Gavin Smithers is a private tutor, covering Broadway, Chipping Campden and the north Cotswolds. He has an English degree from Oxford University and a passion for helping others to discover the joy and satisfaction of great literature.

Gavin's Guides are short books packed with insight. Their key aim is to help you raise your grade! Ask for more information at grnsmithers@hotmail.co.uk

14815263R00081

Printed in Great Britain
by Amazon.co.uk, Ltd.,
Marston Gate.